The Rebuilder:

Principles for Rebuilding Broken Lives, Churches, and
Communities

Christopher A. Lewis

Renown Publishing

The Rebuilder / Christopher A. Lewis
ISBN-13: 978-1-945793-74-5
ISBN-10: 1-945793-74-0

Praise for *The Rebuilder* by Christopher A. Lewis

This erudite piece of work by Bishop Christopher Lewis is both scholarly in its articulation and practical in its application. *The Rebuilder* truly captures the experiences of someone who has exemplified the very principles of the progression from survival to significance. It is one thing to learn by our matriculation through educational institutions, but it is so much more impactful and authentic when learning comes through the daily experiences of life. This is the very context of this book. Real and riveting.

The workbook section at the end of the chapter provides for a deeper interaction with the material, and consequently gives the reader practical and hands on insights that are easily transferrable to their unique context. For every pastor, leader, or learner seeking to make that shift from survival to significance and from maintenance to missional, this is the book for you.

Well done, Bishop Lewis!

Dr. Kwame A. Gilbert
Director of Education and Ministerial Development, Eastern Canada

The Rebuilder is inspiring from the start, giving keys to the future to help understand the discourse of the past, alongside the promising hope of a new narrative for life and church reconstruction. With great depth and clarity, Christopher A. Lewis reveals the essence and paradox of the rebuilding principles which bring hope for broken lives and congregations by shifting them from survival, to success, to significance, to the supernatural.

David E. Ramirez, D.Min.
Assistant General Overseer, and Divisional Director of Education

The Rebuilder is a book of experience. Born in the fires of adversity, this volume's message rises like a phoenix from the ashes. The writer is no novice, the concepts are time tested, the vision is clear, and the outcomes are credible. Read its gripping pages and gain wisdom like Solomon, inspiration like David, and passion like Joshua. Allow the Holy Spirit to apply the illumination of these chapters and paragraphs to your heart, and infuse the practical, proven concepts into your mind.

Wayne C Solomon, D.Min.
Transformed Life Ministries

Christopher Lewis's book, *The Rebuilder*, is a must-read for those who have been given the call to rebuild churches or help those with broken lives. Pastor Lewis shares his insights from twenty-five years of ministry to show ministers how to build, restore, and continue to have faith throughout the process. I would recommend this book to anyone who is looking for a life-altering change in their personal lives and ministry.

Dr. Michael D. Reynolds

Director of Ministerial Development and School of Ministry Project Director of Lilly National Initiative and Church of God International Offices

This book, *The Rebuilder*, is a chronicle of Pastor Christopher's experiences that he documented to help pastors, leaders, and communities that are struggling to rise above our new cultural norms and challenges. With the decline of our young people's interest in the things of God, we need the principles that are trapped within the pages of this book to beat, destroy, and totally annihilate the plans of the evil one.

The statistics on the failures of churches across the nation are terrifying, especially to the young pastors and leaders. Churches across the nation are closing their doors at an estimated rate of between 7,000 and 10,000 churches per year, and around 85 percent of churches have plateaued. But this is only minor statistic in the face of the God-given, time-tested principles in this book. This manuscript was lowered from heaven and was designed to create a new history for your church and community.

Whatever the statistical numbers are, they are no match for what you are about to read. In this amazing book, you will find simple principles that you can immediately apply to your church and community to take it back from the enemy hands. If you're a pastor or leader of a church who has stepped into a broken, helpless, or dysfunctional ministry with the challenge to restore and bring healing to this brokenness, you have just picked up the right book.

R. Pepe Ramnath, PhD
UN-EO (NGO) Ambassador, Research Scientist
Pastor of Miramar Kingdom Community Church

A church split, a failed leader, changing economics, or an aging congregation—there are many reasons for a church to be struggling and in decline. In fact, of the approximately 350,000 churches in the U.S., far more are in need of a major turnaround than are healthy and growing. In this invaluable toolkit filled with effective strategies, principles, and insights, Rev. Christopher Lewis brings hope to struggling churches. This book should be a ministry companion for every pastor and church leader.

Dr. Clifton Clarke
Assistant Provost of William Pannell Center for African American Church Studies
Associate Professor of Black Church Studies and World Christianity Fuller Theological Seminary
Religion and Culture Group Leader Society for Pentecostal Studies

To my mother, Ruth: Thank you for unselfish love, unrelenting prayers, and for the undeniable sacrifices you've made to afford me an education and for supporting my relationship with Jesus.

To my amazing wife and best friend, Annie, my son, Alex, and my daughter, Christiana, and her husband, Vincent: You are my everything, and it's because of your love, prayers, support, and willingness to follow me wherever God assigns me to do His will. Because of your selflessness, I am a better husband, father, and leader.

To all of my five beautiful and generous sisters—Penny, Eserene, Nathalie, Othis, and Prudence—and two adventurous brothers, Joel and Everton: You have all helped to shape me into the man I am today by your love, sacrifices, and support, especially in the building of God's kingdom.

To my mentor, the late T.L. Lowery; my spiritual father and mother, Philip and Alvera Payne; my covenant brother, Kwame Gilbert, and the special people who have shared this journey with me over the past twenty-five years, beginning at Harvestime, Victory Worship Center, and Christian Community: a big thank you!

CONTENTS

Engaging the Proper Tools for Rebuilding—
A Foreword by Dr. Timothy Hill

In all the time that I've known Pastor Christopher A. Lewis, he has been a builder, a builder of people and churches. He builds with careful attention to a master plan, following every detail of the master architect's specifications. As a result, Christopher Lewis has celebrated multiple accomplishments and victories for which he completely gives all glory to God. Every tool he uses serves a meaningful purpose and brings about an intended result. How important it is that we understand that a toolbox should contain many tools with multiple uses, and then appreciate the use of each one. I've heard it said that "if all we have in our toolbox is a hammer, we will treat everything like a nail."

Modern-day Israeli archaeologists have discovered that most excavation sites of ancient cities of the Holy Land come with multiple layers of sediment, ashes, and crushed stone, representing thousands of years of destruction and rebuilding of cities on the same location. Scientists can study centuries—even millennia—of civilizations by sifting through the pieces of homes, tools, and housewares.

In *The Rebuilder*, the perils and triumphs of contemporary ministry are explored in an effort to equip pastors, laypersons and leaders with the proper "toolbox" for rebuilding. The job in a local church may call for a symbolic hammer and nail to secure a "loose board," while the more challenging ministry obstacles, such as a church split or pastoral breach of trust might require numerous tools to deconstruct and shore up what was once a firm foundation.

Author Christopher A. Lewis offers candid and personal illustrations that offer practical examples of rebuilding in the modern church environment. These include pulling up stakes from a comfortable home and stability of ministry to an inner-city store-front with no financial coverage. *The Rebuilder* offers heavy-duty tools, forged through real-life experiences to fend off any resurgence of a wrecking ball that could arise in the restoration process. While no assignment or calling to repair or rebuild comes with a guarantee of success, the tools offered in *The Rebuilder* can be a tool belt to gird about the waist of a prospective church planter or ministry restorer offering biblical helps and experiential testimonies.

—**Dr. Timothy Hill**
General Overseer, Church of God, Cleveland Tennessee

INTRODUCTION

A Need for Rebuilding

The statistics are daunting. Churches across the nation are closing their doors forever. Some estimate that between 7,000 and 10,000 churches will close this year.[1] Others say that number is closer to 4,000 or 5,000.[2] Whatever the number, the message is clear: churches are struggling, ministries are failing.

We also know that 85% of churches are plateauing [3] and that young people continue to leave the church—presumably forever.[4] Unless something changes.

After twenty-five years of evangelistic and pastoral ministry, church planting and community growth on two different continents, this book was born out of a deep burden and need to see healing brought to unhealthy and broken churches beginning in the United States. If you've picked up this book, my guess is this is a burden you share.

If you're a pastor or a leader of a church that is currently struggling to thrive, or if you feel called by the Holy Spirit to step into a broken or dysfunctional ministry in order to restore the body of Christ, this book was written with you in mind.

Serving three different congregations on two different continents has been a great honor and privilege for my wife, Annie, and me for over twenty-five years. As the senior pastor of these unique churches, I have witnessed God's unrelenting love for His people and supernatural care for His church, despite their complexities, stubbornness, and brokenness. I'm familiar with some of the struggles and the concerns you may be wrestling with as you wonder if you're the right person for this particular spiritual battle in this season of life. And make no mistake, this is a spiritual battle. Whenever you are anointed to build something significant in life, you must be spiritually prepared with a double anointing for the inevitable spiritual, physical, emotional and relational battles. In Mathew's Gospel, after Peter's declaration of Jesus as the Messiah at Caesarea Philippi, Jesus made it crystal clear to his disciples when he said, "I will build my church, and the gates of Hades shall not prevail against it" (Matthew 16:18). Note carefully that Jesus never said that the gates of Hades will not try. They will always try, but will never prevail. Therefore, when you carry a burden from the Lord to rebuild and repair His church, be prepared for an adventure of a lifetime. I have come to realize that the enormity and intensity of the burden someone carries is an indication of the level of spiritual battles ahead.

A man with a cushy job named Nehemiah, the cupbearer to the king, found himself in a similar situation and was burdened to return to the devastated city of Jerusalem in order to rebuild her walls and restore her people. I am not sure that when God calls you and gives you a burden for a specific task that you are allowed to say no. How can you say "no" to the One that created you and equipped you to do what only you were born to do? This blueprint is laid out for us in the book that bears the cupbearer's name, Nehemiah 2:1–20.

By looking at the life of this leader, I'll share with you some simple, yet profound truths on how to plan, rebuild, repair and transform dying churches and ministries. I'll also offer personal examples from my own experiences of working alongside churches that had the potential to live but were withering away. At the end of each chapter, a workbook section will give you practical tools to work through this rebuilding and restoration journey in your own ministry context. You will be able to inspire those around you and leave a legacy for the next generation by living out the words of the prophet Isaiah who said, (Isaiah 58:12 NKJV), "You shall be called the Repairer of the Breach, The Restorer of Streets to Dwell In" (Isaiah 58:12).

In this book we'll discuss:

1. The unstoppable power of prayer and fasting.
2. How to plan a successful mission.
3. Successful strategies for managing resources.
4. Protecting your flock from extortionists.
5. Motivating your team toward significant change.
6. Preparing for internal and external opposition and challenges.

7. Maintaining your joy and strength throughout the process.

God can transform a struggling church or stagnant ministry into one that is thriving and actively bringing life-giving change into its home community. And He can use you to facilitate that change.

Your journey begins now.

CHAPTER ONE

Rising to a Challenge

The words of Nehemiah son of Hakaliah:

In the month of Kislev in the twentieth year, while I was in the citadel of Susa, Hanani, one of my brothers, came from Judah with some other men, and I questioned them about the Jewish remnant that had survived the exile, and also about Jerusalem.

They said to me, "Those who survived the exile and are back in the province are in great trouble and disgrace. The wall of Jerusalem is broken down, and its gates have been burned with fire."

When I heard these things, I sat down and wept. For some days I mourned and fasted and prayed before the God of heaven.
—Nehemiah 1:1–4

Annie and I had been serving as the senior pastors in one of the most culturally diverse churches in Chicago for over twelve years when we made the difficult decision to relocate. We chose to answer the call and accepted a new pastoral appointment, relocating our family to one of our sister churches in Florida. The wounds of this new church were fresh and deep, and the remaining members were recovering from a very painful church division.

When I'd first heard their unsettling story, I felt compelled by the Holy Spirit to respond. I felt burdened for this church and for its people even though I had never met them. I tried to resist this feeling by dwelling on my comfort in pastoring a successful, multicultural, debt-free church after many years of struggle.

I was enjoying my slice of the American dream, living in Niles, Illinois, one of America's best communities for families.[5] Both of my kids were attending excellent schools and had great friends. My amazing, courageous wife Annie enjoyed the four seasons of the Midwest, especially autumn. Still, I couldn't shake a gnawing feeling that God was calling my family and I to leave all of this behind and move to Florida.

You will never have perfect peace unless you submit to God's will and purpose for your life, and I learned that lesson the hard way. As the urge to move intensified, Annie and I reverted to what we know best: unrelenting fasting and prayer.

Thirteen years prior, we had felt the same burden to move from another very comfortable life in the beautiful suburbs of Fort Washington, Maryland, where I had served as the evangelism director for a megachurch and taught in the Bible college while serving with some of the most loving and gifted leaders I have ever met. We had just bought our first home in one of those beautiful all-American suburban communities, where deer roam the backyard early in the mornings or late afternoons and turtles stroll across the lawn and driveway ever so often.

What had been even lovelier about living in Oxen Hill was the fact that there was hardly any traffic getting to the office—our commute to work was about a five-minute drive. Annie worked in the church's accounting office and absolutely enjoyed it. It didn't hurt that our daughter, Christy, an only child then, attended the private elementary school in the same building at no cost to us. We loved it there.

That was my first impression of America and the church culture that I would eventually embrace as my own. I met a great father, friend, and mentor in the person of Dr. T.L. Lowery, who is now with Jesus. He was the senior pastor of the great National Church of God and also the chancellor of the National Bible College and Seminary.

Then one day, everything changed after I visited the city of Chicago and fell in love with the rich multi-ethnic, multicultural diversity. How would I break the news to my wife and daughter that God was getting ready to take us to a new, strange, and unfamiliar place? How would I break the news to my spiritual father and his son (my pastor)—and to all of the friends and others who loved us and were extremely kind to me and my family? Talk about being between a rock and a hard place.

This is where your emotions meet your devotion. God intervenes with revelation and favor so that His purpose and plans for your life become a reality. It is moments like these when a decision has to be made that interrupts your comfortable and well-manicured life—when God chooses to move you from the safe zone to the faith zone. Indeed, it was that sort of moment. God prepared the way, and we followed his cue to Chicago.

We packed out belongings, rented out our home, and moved to the inner city on the north side of Chicago. This was absolutely different. Not only was it cold, but instead of deer and turtles in the backyard, we were also greeted by alley rats. I vividly remember that as we arrived at the parsonage, our daughter refused to go into the house. To put it nicely, the urban parsonage was quite different from our suburban home, and so was the store-front church building. I have come to realize that God has a unique way of disguising the greater blessing He has for us until our hearts are in the right place to receive it.

Long story short, after three years of challenging circumstances, the breakthrough came, and God used that same store-front church to provide the needed resources to purchase and relocate the church into a beautiful new facility, complete with a parsonage. A $1.6 million investment was made, and we came out completely debt-free.

Sometimes the enemy tries to fool us into thinking that we need to leave a place when things are rough and tough. Many have missed God's best by running away from the challenges and have never witnessed God's transforming glory rebuild, restore, revive, and recalibrate their families, churches, and communities.

Sometimes God takes us through the ridiculous before he brings us into the miraculous. Just before the supernatural breakthrough in Chicago, I remember scooping up excrement early one morning and asking, with tears running down my cheeks, "God, did I miss Your voice?" This didn't make any sense. If my faith crisis wasn't enough, added to it was the frigid Chicago weather that would freeze anything in its path. While I was having a melt-down service in the sewer at the back of the church, my wife and our one-year-old son Alex were waiting in the freezing church office with only a space heater that took forever to heat up the room.

Sometimes people see the glory, but they need to know the story. If God has truly called you to a people and a place, it's because He wants to make you a blessing to that community. God wants to make you a conduit of His un-stoppable power. He wants to ensure that if you move on, then you leave the community in a better condition than you found it.

One of my biggest ministerial pet peeves is how some leaders leave a ministry assignment before moving to an-other. It seems like many people only hear God telling them to leave when all of the financial resources have been depleted, when the spiritual morale is low, or when internal struggle is brewing in that community. They spir-itualize escapism, laziness, and lack of passion with phrases like, "My season here is up," "I feel a shift," or "I hear the Lord saying...."

My precious wife and I have been on this ecclesiastical adventure for over twenty-five years, on two different continents, in three of the world's greatest cities. It has not been easy, and we have the scars and the stars to prove it.

But the journey has been worth every moment. We have decided that wherever God allows us to serve as pas-tors, we will pour our lives into the people there, and when it's time to transition, we will leave the community better than we found it.

By the grace of God, who grants us the desires of our heart, this had been the case when we were in Guyana. We have seen holistic growth and major development, all without debt and financial resources still in the bank.

We applied the same rebuilding principles to the church in Chicago, and they work every time. By the time we were ready to pass the baton to the next person, we left them debt-free, not just with monies in the bank, but with investment CDs and funds that were designated for specific projects.

Let me stick a pin right here, church leaders. I have sometimes heard, and perhaps you have too, that "money follows ministry." I have a slightly different approach.

I believe God supplies the resources for ministries that have proper financial structures and systems in place and are good stewards of those resources. I also believe that churches and leaders should live within their means, being frugal where necessary and wise at all times.

Remember that these are God's resources, not ours. Remember Jesus's parable about the master who told his servant, "You have been faithful with a few things; I will put you in charge of many things" (Matthew 25:23).

Faithfulness is a significant principle for rebuilding the economic power in your life and ministry. Wise investment and spending of God's resources always precedes fruitfulness, abundance, and debt-free living.

Poverty has a way of attracting poverty. But wealth and prosperity, when well managed and used for its intended purpose, can transform nations for the glory of God. King

Solomon was blessed by God with two of the greatest gifts given to humanity: wealth and the wisdom to use it.

I believe Solomon lived debt-free because he owed no one and attracted wealth from other nations without resorting to war. There is a lack of clear evidence that Solomon took Israel to war at all during the course of his reign. I suspect that he used the wisdom God gave him to foster diplomatic relations and international peace, in order to use his resources to build up the Kingdom of God. Wars cost lots and lots of money.

For example, "regarding America's brief involvement in World War I, historians can see that $334 billion was spent fighting the enemy (an amount adjusted to reflect inflation). That amount rose to $4.1 trillion during the Second World War."[6]

Similarly, we have destructive wars in our churches today over music styles, dress codes, denominational badges, ecclesiastical titles and positions, styles of governments, increasing "power distances" in leadership, racial discrimination, and politics. While some of these are necessary, you be the judge. Many of them divide the body of Christ and destroy priceless relationships and friendships in the process.

God has a way of disguising His blessings for your life and ministry until your heart is fully developed to receive it. During our first two years of ministry in Chicago, it was very challenging. The church could not afford to pay me a full salary, but through the kindness of our state administrative bishop, one of our mission-minded sister churches came to my rescue.

One morning, just after a great time of family devotions, I received a phone call from my administrative bishop. He let me know in the kindest words and the most pleasant tones of affirmation that my support would end in about six months and he could not guarantee any further support.

Have you ever been on a water slide? It might take you half an hour or longer to make it to the top, but only seconds for gravity to pull you back to the bottom. That was the reality of the moment for me. In situations like this, you can try to resist, but it happens so quickly that it can leave you feeling incapacitated.

Life consists of many highs and lows, and your ability to navigate wisely through these tough terrains will determine the strength of your character. Just before I hit the bottom of my proverbial water slide, the phone rang again. This time it was a good friend who was serving as the administrative bishop of Canada. After a few pleasantries, he told me that my name was on the short list for a pastoral position in one of the leading churches in Canada. Our conversation ended, and I was at the top of the waterslide again. The thrill I had lost so quickly was back.

I began to sing "I Am Not Forgotten" and "I Am a Friend of God" by Israel Houghton. Was this an answer to prayer? Perhaps we had completed our work in Chicago, but in reality, we had just begun. My thoughts had begun to readjust themselves to accommodate information I had received while my heart followed suit to justify my emotion and placate my feelings.

If you ever find yourself more taken up with the work of the Lord rather than the Lord of the work, ministry can become a drug that creates an insatiable appetite for the thrill of God instead of the will of God. I thought that perhaps, like the prophet Elijah, my brook had dried up because it hadn't been full to begin with. Maybe this was never meant to be a destination but a transition onto something else.

There will be moments in your life when you will question the sovereignty God. Like Jacob, I began wrestling with God's sovereignty as questions flood my mind about his direction for my life, family, and future ministry. What was I to do? Did God really want me to leave my multicultural, debt-free Chicago church family and embark on a new ministry adventure? The grief I felt for this sister church was much like Nehemiah's grief at the state of Israel. I felt compelled—and yet fearful—of what God might be calling me and my family to do.

Clarity produces confidence, but faith creates movement. However, the voice of the Lord became clear. My family and I made the difficult decision to leave the comfort zone of my well-established life and ministry and move eleven hundred miles across the country and into the heart of South Florida.

Upon arriving, it didn't take too long for me to discern the spiritual climate and health of my new church. The people welcomed us with a sunny, south-Florida welcome. But behind some of the smiles, it was if some of them were really saying, "You don't know what you're getting yourselves into." And they were right. We really didn't know what we signed up for. Isn't it just like God to give us the A and Z, but requires us to trust that He will be there through the L-M-N-O-P?

Just like an experienced medical doctor can tell a patient is ill by their demeanor, it was obvious that there was something wrong in this congregation. They were sheep wounded by the experience of losing long-standing and meaningful relationships. But that was just the tip of the iceberg.

Like doctors who diagnose a patient with a few questions and an exam, we dug deeper and found that their trouble was much deeper than what was apparent on the surface. As the days, weeks and months rolled by, we began to uncover other toxic factors like an impending lawsuit. The atmosphere was tense, and the people were scattered everywhere like sheep without a shepherd.

However, the Holy Spirit began to show us the remnant of healthy Christians among the congregation. There was a group of prayer warriors that was praying and fasting for my family before we even arrived. As a believer, I have prayed and fasted all my life, but this group of intercessors challenged my prayer life. It was as if the Holy Spirit was telling me that we would not survive in this place without a perpetual and unrelenting prayer life.

Through their genuine and passionate prayer, these precious saints showed us that they desperately wanted to rebuild the broken-down walls of their church. They just needed a shepherd with a vision to help guide them through this complex and complicated seasons in the life of their church.

Like the woman with the issue of blood in Mark 5:25–34, this body had been hemorrhaging for quite some time. It was clear that the internal bleeding needed to stop immediately before new life and health could be restored. In other words, these brothers and sisters desperately needed to touch the hem of the Great Physician's garment and be made whole again.

When considering the disrepair of the church building itself, I couldn't help but notice another biblical parallel comparable to the returned Jewish exiles in the days of Nehemiah. Their temple and place or worship was broken down and unattractive, in need of physical repair. From the parking lot to the bathrooms to the kitchen, much of the building was undesirable.

This brings me to my second pet peeve concerning ministry leaders. While I believe that each congregation should do their very best to care for their pastor and his family, I have a problem with pastors who live in comfort and are not concerned that the house of God is in ruin.

Why Nehemiah?

The Bible doesn't tell us much about Nehemiah's family heritage, but as we follow his journey through the book that bears his name, we learn a great deal about his character and his devotion to God. Some scholars believe that he was a priest in addition to being the cupbearer to the king.[7] That last title alone speaks volumes about Nehemiah's trustworthiness, as no monarch would give the cupbearer responsibility to a man unless he inspired total trust.

As the cupbearer to King Artaxerxes, one of Nehemiah's primary duties was to taste wine for the king to ensure it was not poisoned. God's favor on his life and the purity of Nehemiah's calling was demonstrated by his proximity to the king.

God knew He would need a man on the inside who could get the necessary permission when it was time to rebuild the walls, and Nehemiah was that man. God had everything set up for Nehemiah to be the man who would salvage Jerusalem and lead God's people toward rebuilding their city walls, reviving their temple for worship of Jehovah and restoring their prestige among the other nations of the world.

God strategically and sovereignly positioned Nehemiah for a specific purpose that would ultimately lead to preserving the seed that would bruise the head of the serpent (Genesis 3:15, Galatians 3:16).

Israel in Disarray

In Nehemiah chapter 1, when Nehemiah greeted his brother, Hanani, and the other men who had come to Susa from Judah, Nehemiah no doubt was anticipating hearing all about the temple restoration project and how the streets of Jerusalem were filled with people buying and selling and building new homes to start new families. Instead, he heard that the walls of the city remained in ruins. That the city lacked any form of protection, and the people were living in fear and disgrace.

Oh, what a blow to the heart that must have been! I can only imagine the flood of emotions and thoughts that must have hit him at once. How he reacted shows the character of Nehemiah.

Commenting on Nehemiah 1:4–11, Derek Kinder wrote, "Since Nehemiah's natural bent was for swift, decisive action, his behavior here is remarkable. It shows where his priority lies. It also reveals, by every phase in this verse, the unhurried and far from superficial backgrounds of the famous 'arrow prayer' of 2:4 and the achievements which were to follow it."[8]

Nehemiah's reaction to the destruction of Jerusalem and its holy places shows his deep commitment to the God of Israel (Nehemiah 1:4). He grieved and wept over the state of his people. Then he repented on their behalf and committed himself to being the leader they so desperately needed.

Throughout his quest to rebuild the wall and reestablish God's people as a nation, Nehemiah demonstrated humility, boldness, and a knowledge of the Scriptures that inspired the people of Israel to renew their dedication as God's people.

Rarely has a person in ancient or modern times taken on such a monumental task with such allegiance to God through every step. Nehemiah believed God Himself would bring about success, which fueled his passion to display God's faithfulness to Israel.

By pointing to God over and over and proving great things could be done through Him, Nehemiah changed the course of history. Even today, his example breathes life into us when our calling seems uncertain and our ministry tenuous. Nehemiah is a leader we can trust, especially when we are tackling a task that seems bigger than our limited human capacity.

Answering the Call

You're probably reading this book because you're a believing member of the body of Christ whose spirit is grieved by brokenness or dysfunction you've witnessed within your nuclear family, your church family, or your community. At times you may feel like Nehemiah, so overwhelmed by what you see. All you can do is cry out to God in repentance, seeking direction.

And as you go to the Lord with your grief, you may find that God is preparing you to take a step out of your place of comfort and into a place of struggle. You may find that He is calling you to step up and be the leader that a broken church or ministry so desperately needs—God is calling you into a ministry of rebuilding, repair, and restoration.

You may have some uncertainty. After all, how can you know for sure that the church on your heart is as broken as you think it is? And how do you know God wants *you* to be the one to rebuild and restore it?

If you're uncertain whether or not the church or ministry God has placed on your heart is in need of a Nehemiah-like experience, here are seven questions to ask yourself:

1. Are you comfortable with your current state of life, ministry, and vocation?
2. Have you been fasting and praying about God's next assignment for your life?
3. Is there a gnawing restlessness in your spirit that won't go away but intensifies every time you pray?

4. If you are married, does your spouse share your burden?

5. If you have children who are in school, what was their reaction when you told them about your burden and what it would entail?

6. Are you confident that you have done your best to fulfill the last ministry assignment?

7. Have you spoken to a friend or a colleague who did what you are burdened to do?

Hopefully, with the help of these questions, you can gain clarity on the church or ministry that you have a burden for.

Let's Rebuild!

In the opening chapter of Nehemiah, we see a man who has genuine concern for others, but more than that, we see a man who seeks after the Lord's heart. A man who recognizes his own sin and the sin of his people, and who comes to the Lord with a broken and repentant heart seeking to be reconciled and restored.

Like Joseph and Daniel before him, Nehemiah was raised up in the eyes of a foreign king specifically for a task that the Lord had prepared far in advance. A task that would bring healing and restoration to the people of Israel, and through her, to the rest of the world.

This is why Nehemiah is such a powerful picture of what it takes to be the leader that broken churches so desperately need. His example guided me as I worked to restore the Lauderhill church, and I believe God wants to use Nehemiah's story to help you as you take on your own church project so desperately in need of repair.

We're going to look at eight restoration principles that you can put into place to repair brokenness and lead a church toward renewed life. As you implement these principles and reflect on the life of Nehemiah, you can trust that God will guide you along the way. He will provide what is needed to rebuild His walls.

WORKBOOK

Chapter One Questions

Question: What overall church trends do you find most disturbing? Do you feel an overwhelming burden from the Lord to specifically address any of these current trends through your life and ministry?

_____

_____

_____

_____

_____

_____

_____

_____

_____

Question: What specific church situation(s) has the Lord put on your heart (and perhaps in your life)? If you were a "church doctor," what diagnosis would you make of this particular church?

_____

_____

_____

_____

_____

_____

_____

_____

_____

Question: In what areas are the walls of protection broken down in this church? Where is this church most vulnerable?

_____

_____

_____

_____

_____

_____

_____

_____

_____

Question: What changes in your life are you willing and/or able to make to be used by God for the restoration of this church (or of His church as a whole)?

_____

_____

_____

_____

_____

_____

_____

_____

_____

Question: In what ways has God uniquely prepared you, as He did Nehemiah, for a ministry of rebuilding and restoration? In what ways does the task before you exceed your human capacity? How have you (or will you) depend completely on God for the restoration of His church?

_____

_____

_____

_____

_____

_____

_____

_____

_____

_____

_____

_____

Question: *Nehemiah demonstrated humility, boldness, and a knowledge of the Scriptures.* In what ways can a prideful leader destroy a struggling church? Why is boldness so essential when dealing with internal and external conflict? How can a clear, scriptural foundation restore a congregation's hope and confidence?

_____

_____

_____

_____

_____

_____

_____

_____

_____

_____

_____

Action: Just as Nehemiah set aside a specific time to seek God and His will in the desperate needs of Jerusalem, you should commit to a time of seeking God before proceeding to take action.

When and for what length of time will you pray and seek God's will for the situation on your heart?

What specific days in the next month will you set aside as prayer retreats (see next chapter for more on prayer and fasting)?

What quality or qualities from the life of Nehemiah will you intentionally study and work to develop, so that you can be the leader God and a broken church need you to be?

Chapter One Notes

CHAPTER TWO

Rebuilding the Heart

When I heard these things, I sat down and wept. For some days I mourned and fasted and prayed before the God of heaven...

"Lord, let your ear be attentive to the prayer of this your servant and to the prayer of your servants who delight in revering your name. Give your servant success today by granting him favor in the presence of this man."

—Nehemiah 1:4, 11

If you've ever been the fan of a losing sports team, then you probably know what it's like to be looking from the outside in and feeling as though you have a better handle than the coaches do on what the team needs to be doing differently. You can quickly identify the players who need an attitude check and the plays that just aren't working. You can name a handful of instances in which the coaches made the wrong call, and you have a few ideas of what the right call would have been.

When we're in this kind of position, on the outside looking in, it's easy to have all the answers. It's easy to want to establish ourselves as experts, but the reality is we really don't know the deep-rooted issues that are going on to cause the team—or spouse, or business, or child—to act in such a way.

Nehemiah understood this. From his point of view, the situation in Jerusalem may have seemed pretty obvious—the people needed to repent and return to God, building the city as they did so—yet his response wasn't to show up and take charge, bossing people around and making assumptions about how they had found themselves in such a predicament.

His response was to step back and seek God. Not only did Nehemiah want to observe the situation for himself, but he also resolved to personal intercession and fasting before ever taking a step in the direction of Jerusalem.

I am convinced that spiritual rebuilding has to start first within the walls of human hearts before it can happen anywhere else. Drawing from Nehemiah's words in 1:11, and my personal experience from over twenty years of pastoral ministry, I am persuaded that unrelenting prayer, coupled with fasting and strategic planning, must precede every assignment we undertake in life, especially in the context of Christian ministry.

Rebuilding Principle #1:
Keep God at the Center of Everything from Start to Finish

LORD, the God of heaven, the great and awesome God, who

keeps his covenant of love with those who love him and
keep his commandments, let your ear be attentive and
your eyes open to hear the prayer your servant is praying
before you day and night for your servants, the people of
Israel. I confess the sins we Israelites, including myself and
my father's family, have committed against you. We have
acted very wickedly toward you. We have not obeyed the
commands, decrees and laws you gave your servant Moses.
—Nehemiah 1:5–7

When we look at Nehemiah's approach to prayer in Nehemiah 1:4–7, we see a similarity in how Jesus instructed his own disciples on prayer in Matthew 6:9–13. This approach is incredibly powerful, and implementing it will possibly change the way that you commune with God and seek His will. It has transformed my own life, and it certainly helped bring clarity as I sought God for what He was calling me to do at this church.

This prayer approach begins with the acknowledgement of who God is: "LORD, the God of heaven, the great and awesome God, who keeps his covenant of love with those who love him and keep his commandments" (Nehemiah 1:5).

Theologian Hugh G.M. Williamson notes that the elaborate opening deliberately postponed Nehemiah's cry for help and instead pointed more immediately to heaven.[9] This focused the prayer on God, rather than focusing on Nehemiah's needs and struggles.

The prayer continues with a time of confession, followed by Nehemiah reminding God of his faithfulness and covenants with Israel. Williamson notes that Nehemiah's awareness of God's promises and attributes allowed him to boldly ask for things with the expectation that God would deliver (Nehemiah 1:9).[10]

It is in this spirit of humble-boldness that Nehemiah was then able to request in verses ten and eleven that God grant him favor in the eyes of the ruler and authorities He has placed over Nehemiah and His people. On this final aspect of Nehemiah's prayer, Charles Fenmen writes, "In the eyes of the world, Artaxerxes was an important person, a man with influence, who could decide on life or death," but in the eyes of Nehemiah, this powerful Persian King was just another man—no match for Yahweh.[11]

For me, this persistent prayer approach of worshipping God, confessing sin, reminding God of his promises, and requesting his favor and help, was the backbone of the turnaround in this church. Before I arrived in Florida, I spent countless hours on my knees, seeking God and getting my heart in the right place. I was on the twenty-fourth day of my annual twenty-one days of fasting and prayer when I received a phone call to inform me that I was considered a possible candidate for the pastoral position at this church.

So, the first ministry teams that were established were a prayer and fasting team and a team of dedicated prayer leaders. Prayer times were appointed, which has not changed since, but has grown "glo-cally," meaning both locally and globally.

We began every morning, Monday through Friday, with an hour of prayer on a conference prayer line where church members and friends from around the city, state, and world could call in to pray with us and for us. In addition, we held a Monday evening prayer meeting at the church.

During our annual twenty-one days of prayer and fasting, we pray around the clock and these same leaders that started out with me are the one maintaining effectiveness and "glo-cal" impact. As a result, many more were added from other churches and denominations, including pastors and bishops.

One the most beautiful stories I love to share about the impact of the prayer line ministry is the fact that God used it to divinely connect a lovely couple who are now married and serving as leaders in our church. I had the privilege of performing their wedding ceremony, and I am honored to be their pastor.

This focus on prayer was invaluable. It changed many broken hearts and continues to be the fuel for our church's continued health, growth, and community impact. It allowed us to hear God's voice, and it put us on the path of restoration.

Rebuilding Principle #2:
Pray and Fast

They are your servants and your people, whom you redeemed by your great strength and your mighty hand. Lord, let your ear be attentive to the prayer of this your servant and to the prayer of your servants who delight in revering your name. Give your servant success today by granting him favor in the presence of this man.
—Nehemiah 1:10–11

While prayer is a great way to get your heart and the hearts of God's people in the right place, there is a certain supernatural power behind fasting. Nehemiah knew this, as verse four says that he "mourned and fasted" for days after he heard the news about Jerusalem.

Fasting doesn't have to be complicated or elaborate. It doesn't need thirty or twenty or even ten days before it "takes effect." The simplest fasting routine can make just as big of an impact as the more extensive fasting commitments. The key is to implement something that is doable—something you can adhere to.

Spiritual sacrifices that seek to please God and not man to bring you to a place where physical hunger and spiritual hunger intersect. Jesus said it best to his disciples: "Blessed are those to hunger and thirst for righteousness, for they will be filled" (Matthew 5:6).

There is a prayer and fasting culture at our church now that has cross-pollinated other churches across the city, country, and globe. We observed a time of fasting and prayer every Thursday from 10 a.m. to 2 p.m. The basic rules were to abstain from food during that day and to commit to the time of prayer. People could come and go as their schedules allowed. Staff members were expected to participate in prayer for one hour.

We made it simple. We made it easy to follow. And amazingly, the Thursday prayer and fasting service has become the largest praying group of all the prayer meetings in our church, and it continues to grow weekly. If you really want to see your family, church, and community thrive, you must subscribe to an intentional lifestyle of passionate prayer and fasting. I believe Solomon was in the supernatural realm when he prophesied to Israel, reminding them of God's abiding presence with his covenant people: "If my people, who are called by my name, will humble themselves and pray and seek my face and turn from their wicked ways then I will hear from heaven and I will forgive their sin and will heal their land" (2 Chronicles 7:14).

A Matter of the Heart

I was born with what's known as a ventricular septal defect (or VSD). This means I had a hole in my heart when I was born, and I wasn't expected to live long unless it was corrected. The only way to treat a heart defect like mine was with open-heart surgery. However being born in Guyana, South America, in the '70s without health insurance and with poor health care didn't give me much of a change. I was at the top of the child with special needs list, yet the only thing many could offer me was a kind smile laced with sympathy.

Apparently, my funeral was planned every year by everyone who knew about my condition. From primary school to high school, I was told that I should never attempt anything strenuous like sports, but I did it all anyway. I figured we were all going to die someday anyway, so if I died, let me go out with a bang doing the things I enjoyed. I loved soccer, swimming, fast cars, jet skis, and motorcycles, and I did it all.

How did I manage to defy the odds that were stacked up against me? You see, my mother is a prayer warrior.

As a single mother of eight children, she had no other choice but prayer many days in order to feed us. She told me that when I was around the age of four or five, she noticed that I was a bit pale for some time. She took me to a Pentecostal church in the village where we lived, and the pastor and prayer team anointed me with olive oil until I looked like greasy pole at the county fair. Then they laid hands on me and prayed in all kinds of different languages that she did not understand until God told them to stop. They prayed so loud and so long that she believes I fell asleep on the church bench.

Even though it sounds humorous and always makes me laugh, I know now that it was the Holy Spirit that empowered those women in that little country church to anoint me and pray God's abundant life and purpose into my abnormal heart.

During my early pastoral years in Guyana, I was privileged to have met and prayed for that pastor who took the time to pray all night for a five-year-old boy with a severe heart condition. That boy go the opportunity to preach the gospel to her. Is anything too hard for the Lord?

Even so, for thirty-seven years I had never heard my heartbeat, and neither had my wife, my kids, or my doctors. My heart has always sounded like a race car, due to the blood gushing from one ventricle to the other. There is no logical explanation for why I am still alive, because very few people ever survive to adulthood with a major unrepaired VSD.

But at age thirty-eight, after my heart spent all that time attempting to repair itself, I heard a sweet, unfamiliar sound coming from the inside of my chest. The sound of a racecar running out of gas now sounds like perfectly timed drops of rain. I know Who was responsible for keeping my alive all those years until my heart was repaired. God is our healer, and He wants to sustain you the same way He did me. He wants your family and church to thrive.

Prayer and fasting are key elements to prepare the heart for a life in the will and work of God. These principles should be used privately before you launch into your restoration ministry, and they should also become the core strategy of any congregation that desires change and repair.

Remember, a church that is unwilling to pray and fast together is a church that will not stand for long. God desires to fulfill His promises to His people; He wants nothing more than to pour out blessings, uncommon favor and unconditional love upon his church. He often demonstrates his love through supernatural healings, miracles, and divine opportunities to bring hope and restoration.

Unless a broken church is willing to come to the cross in repentance and humility, nothing will change. To be more specific, nothing will change for the better. The apostle Paul used the human body as a metaphor to describe the anatomy and functionality of the church (1 Corinthians 12:12–27).

What he didn't focus much on here was that the body ages, grows weary, needs lots care and repair, and has to be sustained and maintained in order to function at its maximal potential. Olympians and other professional athletes understand this principle best, because their lives and careers depend on it.

So whether your ministry is healthy or on life support, you must be intentional or else your body will degenerate. The apostle Paul, who was so mightily used of God and was given the assignment to write half of the New Testament, reminds us with these sobering words: "I discipline my body like an athlete, training it to do what it should. Otherwise, I fear that after preaching to others I myself might be disqualified" (1 Corinthians 9:27 NLT).

WORKBOOK

Chapter Two Questions

Question: Describe a time when you assumed you understood a problem in ministry, only to learn more insights later that changed your perspective. What can you learn from that experience?

_____

_____

_____

_____

_____

_____

_____

_____

_____

Question: What does it mean to be teachable? Why is this so important for leaders? How do you remain teachable, yet confident?

_____

_____

_____

_____

_____

_____

_____

_____

_____

Question: What is your experience with the spiritual discipline of fasting? What did you learn from that, and how did God use the experience?

_____

_____

_____

_____

_____

_____

_____

Action for Individuals: For one week, structure your prayer time as Nehemiah did.

Worship. Compile a list (or index cards) of Scriptures, names of God, worship songs, and so forth to focus your heart on who God is—His character and attributes.

Confess sin. Again, use the Word to examine your heart. Look at the lists in Galatians 5 and Colossians 3 contrasting the works of the flesh and the fruit of the Spirit. Reread the principles of the Sermon on the Mount to see the heart-attitudes of a follower of Christ.

Remind God of His promises. To remind God of His promises, you must know and claim them. What specific promises of God's Word apply to the current situation you are facing? Ask God to reveal a few specific promises that will encourage you and the congregation throughout this rebuilding process.

Request His favor and help. What is it that you want to see God do in and through this church? Do not pray, "God, bless this ministry." Instead, have specific requests, but realize that God often chooses to answer in His own ways, and leave the details of the execution to Him.

Action for Pastors/Church Leaders: Once you have established your personal prayer time, make arrangements for a corporate fast.

1. When will you pray together?
2. How long will the meetings be?

3. Will there be a prayer meeting specific for the leadership and another one for the congregation as a whole?
4. Who outside of the situation will commit to praying for you and for the church?
5. What will you fast from? (e.g., fast from all food, a fast from specific types of foods as in Daniel 1, or a fast from social media or entertainment)?
6. Be intentional to train, equip, and appoint prayer leaders.

Note: Some members of the church may have medical/personal concerns preventing them from total abstinence from food—be sure to make allowances that encourage them to still participate in the fast in a safe manner.

Chapter Two Notes

.

CHAPTER THREE

Rebuilding Health

I went to Jerusalem, and after staying there three days I set out during the night with a few others. I had not told anyone what my God had put in my heart to do for Jerusalem. There were no mounts with me except the one I was riding on.

By night I went out through the Valley Gate toward the Jackal Well and the Dung Gate, examining the walls of Jerusalem, which had been broken down, and its gates, which had been destroyed by fire. Then I moved on toward the Fountain Gate and the King's Pool, but there was not enough room for my mount to get through; so I went up the valley by night, examining the wall. Finally, I turned back and reentered through the Valley Gate.
—Nehemiah 2:11–15

Facebook, the large social media website, ran into a bit of trouble not too long ago when it was discovered that the site was selling user data.[12] The quick fix, of course, was to apologize for what had happened and stop selling the data. But the damage had been done; it was a public relations nightmare. Users' trust of Facebook plummeted, and the company is still trying to recover from the blow.

What happened to Facebook is a great example of how the internal and external health of a church is affected when things go wrong. It's not enough to repair the inner workings (leadership, finances, etc.). You'll find that you also need to repair the external relationships, too.

It starts with assessing the damage, internally and externally, and doing what needs to be done to stop the bleeding and restore health.

Nehemiah discovered a state of disrepair and squabbling upon his arrival in Jerusalem. However, rather than jumping right into the task of rebuilding the wall, he took three days to familiarize himself with the people of Jerusalem, and then, without any fanfare or promises of restoring the city to her former glory, he slipped out in the cover of darkness with a handful of others to take in all the of the damage before coming back to the people with a plan to move forward.

Restoring Jerusalem would be no easy task. Theologian Frank E. Gaebelein points out that "the walls and gates of Jerusalem had lain in ruins since their destruction by Nebuchadnezzar some 130 years before, despite attempts to rebuild them. The leaders and the people had evidentially become reconciled to this sad state of affair."[13]

Nehemiah knew that the issue of the physical wall was just one of the many aspects of brokenness that existed in Jerusalem. He understood that to restore the city and the people to full health, he needed a plan that brought the people together, restored faith in the city, and then physically rebuilt what had been torn down.

Nehemiah's approach of first getting a handle on the dynamics and demographics of the communities within the city before he could better evaluate the situation and plan for the re-construction and re-instruction of the broken-down walls, gates, and people of Jerusalem, is one of the best examples of what it takes to get an incarnational restoration ministry off the ground.

Rebuilding Principle #3:
Tackle the Day to Day

If you are stepping into a ministry that is in an advanced state of disrepair, it's vital that you have a full understanding of how the previous leaders handled its day-to-day management. This includes financial obligations such as monthly bills, mortgages, taxes, and payroll.

The church I stepped into was all but drowning in debt. One of the first steps I took was contacting the creditors in order to refinance the church's mortgage and lower the monthly insurance premiums. It was during this process that we discovered that the church had three liens placed against it by the city of Lauderhill.

These liens had been accruing additional penalties for over a decade. They were there because the church had neglected to repair and maintain its property, especially the parking lot and landscaping. Not only did the fines make it impossible to refinance the mortgage but also the amount of the liens was all but impossible for our small and struggling congregation to ever hope to repay.

This new and unexpected turn of events caught most (but not all) of the remaining congregation by surprise. It also led me into a series of difficult conversations with individuals, including some who had remained with the church and others who had left, about the state of the church's current financial crisis. No one, including the former pastor, was willing to accept responsibility for the poor financial planning that had led to the debt in which we found ourselves.

What should have led to our church's ruin however afforded our small remnant to come together in prayer and engage with the leaders in our community to find a mutually acceptable repayment plan for the monies we owed to the city.

Tackling big internal problems, such as crippling debt, can be overwhelming for any person trying to repair a broken church. After all, there is nothing heartening about peeling back the layers and discovering the ugly reality of your situation.

However, God can turn these places of pain into opportunities for the congregation to come together. And from what I've found, the direr the situation, the more determined the congregation tends to become—if they are rooted in prayer and fasting, of course.

Rebuilding Principle #4:
Build Trust and Attract Greater Support from Your Home Community

Then I said to them, "You see the trouble we are in: Jerusalem lies in ruins, and its gates have been burned with fire.

*Come, let us rebuild the wall of Jerusalem, and we will no
longer be in disgrace. I also told them about the gracious
hand of my God on me and what the king had said to me.*
—Nehemiah 2:17–18

Another aspect of assessing the damage involves getting the congregation to see the problem *and then commit to change*. As a pastor, I carry a perpetual burden for the people I am privileged to serve as well as for the spiritual and social needs of the community and city at large—especially for those who have never met and accepted Christ as their personal Savior. As a result, one of my first tasks upon arriving in my new community was not just evaluating the internal health of the church I'd stepped into, but the health of its relationship with the city of Lauderhill.

It was clear to me that only a miracle from God and the forgiveness and favor of the city of Lauderhill could turn the fate of our church from hopelessness to hopefulness. Again, God used our situation as a catalyst to motivate and redirect the church into accelerated action, shifting the entire congregation into a new mindset, which propelled me to schedule an emergency city hall meeting to explain our financial plight and beg for mercy.

When my opportunity came to speak, I presented the social and economic conditions of the church to a board of seven city officials, including the city's mayor. From the expressions on their faces, I could see that they all seemed appalled by the information, yet only one city manager spoke up in our favor and gave me some assurance that they were appreciative of our pledge to cure the problems and bring every violation up to compliance with city regulations and codes.

I left that meeting feeling confident that the city was now our ally, and that though the officials had been frustrated by our past behavior, they wanted to work with us. But I could also tell that their actions would be contingent upon our due diligence in proving that the church was an asset to the community rather than a liability.

Without delay, and with much prayer and planning, we embarked on an urgent stewardship campaign called "Operation Parking Lot." I was sensitive to the present financial condition of the people in the church and sought for assistance from outside sources. In turn, God softened those hearts toward us and, with some help from leadership within our church conference/denomination, we were able to secure an advance on a loan and raise enough funds to fully repair and bring our parking lot up to code within two months.

After the parking lot was completed and dedicated, there was an immediate difference in the atmosphere and attitude of the congregation. It was evident from the financial response of the congregation before and after the completion of this project that they were motivated to rebuild their church again. There was also a fresh excitement again among the remnant members. This energy became contagious, attracting new people as well as some former members back to the church.

God also granted us favor with the city. The officials reduced our debt from hundreds of thousands of dollars to only a few hundred. This not only restored our name but it gave us credibility within our community that would allow us future opportunities to partner with the people of our city to serve those in need.

Bringing Ultimate Health

Restoring a church or ministry means so much more than simply growing the congregation. It means healing *everything* that is broken. It means tackling that debt, fixing that parking lot, remodeling bathrooms and nurseries and ultimately restoring relationships with each other and the community. Nehemiah knew this.

To paraphrase theologian Harold L. Willmington, Nehemiah inspected the wall first. Then he met with the leaders. Then he went out alone and at night for even more inspections. Then he again met with leaders. Finally, when he urged them to rebuild, he had such a clear understanding of the state of things that he was able to win over the people and get them on board with his simple but strategic plan to rebuild the wall.[14]

This approach takes time. It will require you to look at the big picture *and* the minute details. It will force you to fix the crumbling church building while at the same time fixing crumbling hearts. Years of hard work and smart decisions have slowly but surely made a difference. Our back debt has been miraculously cancelled or paid in full, and we were able to add one more full-time staff member to our team. In addition to our parking lot restoration project, we have since remodeled our bathrooms, kitchen, nursery, fellowship hall, sanctuary, and stage and have given a facelift to the foyer and green room.

The goal is complete restoration, inside and out. For a truly restored church is one that is healthy from its budget to its relationship with the community it serves.

WORKBOOK

Chapter Three Questions

Question: What is your understanding of the problems facing your church? Who are key people from the church's past and present who can help you understand the problems?

_____

_____

_____

_____

_____

_____

_____

_____

_____

Question: How can you gather further needed information and insight in a manner that will not encourage division, gossip, or strife?

_____

_____

_____

_____

_____

_____

_____

_____

_____

_____

Question: How would you rate the church's strength in the following areas?

Finances
    1. Debt vs. income?
    2. Are there past-due bills? Unpaid staff?

Staff
    1. Over- or understaffed?
    2. How is morale among the staff?
    3. Are there factions within the congregation supporting different staff members?

4. Is each staff member contributing to the problems or combatting them?

Building and Grounds
1. Are there safety concerns?
2. Clean or cluttered?
3. Old and dated vs. fresh and welcoming?
4. Is the space appropriate (not too crowded, but not so empty that it adds to the despair)?
5. Are sound and technology equipment in good working order?
6. Is there proper signage out front?
7. Is there trimmed landscaping and a welcoming exterior?
8. Do you have a well-trained team in place paid or volunteers that is responsible for the general upkeep and maintenance of the grounds and facilities?

_____

_____

_____

_____

_____

_____

_____

_____

_____

_____

_____

_____

Question: What is the church's relationship to the community? For example, do you aid those in need? Do you pray for and support local law enforcement and government leaders? What are you known for in the community? Are you involved in legal violations or financial ruin? Are your buildings and grounds an eyesore?

_____

_____

_____

_____

_____

_____

_____

_____

_____

_____

_____

Action: Looking over the assessments that you have made, sit down with the church leadership and come up with a list of the most pressing external problems (logistics, finances, facilities) and the most pressing internal problems (division, moral issues, discouragement). Try to keep the lists between five and seven different concerns.

Prayerfully put each list in order of which needs that God would have you to address first, second, etc. Then write out an action plan for how you will present each need to the congregation and involve the entire church in working toward rebuilding, restoration, and revival.

Make note if there are any community leaders who could come alongside to help the church—or be helped by the church. One of the secrets to your church's success with the community is a positive relationship with the schools in the community. You can begin by honoring the teachers on a special day.

Chapter Three Notes

_____

_____

_____

_____

_____

_____

_____

_____

_____

_____

_____

_____

_____

_____

_____

_____

_____

_____

_____

_____

_____

CHAPTER FOUR

Rebuilding Leadership

Ezra the teacher of the Law stood on a high wooden platform built for the occasion. Beside him on his right stood Mattithiah, Shema, Anaiah, Uriah, Hilkiah and Maaseiah; and on his left were Pedaiah, Mishael, Malkijah, Hashum, Hashbaddanah, Zechariah and Meshullam.

Ezra opened the book. All the people could see him because he was standing above them; and as he opened it, the people all stood up. Ezra praised the LORD, the great God; and all the people lifted their hands and responded, "Amen! Amen!" Then they bowed down and worshiped the LORD with their faces to the ground.

The Levites—Jeshua, Bani, Sherebiah, Jamin, Akkub, Shabbethai, Hodiah, Maaseiah, Kelita, Azariah, Jozabad, Hanan and Pelaiah—instructed the people in the Law while the people were standing there. They read from the Book of the Law of God, making it clear and giving the meaning so that the people understood what was being read.

Then Nehemiah the governor, Ezra the priest and teacher of the Law, and the Levites who were instructing the people said to them all, "This day is holy to the LORD your God. Do not mourn or weep." For all the people had been weeping as they listened to the words of the Law.
—Nehemiah 8:4–9

When a church is broken, the leadership is oftentimes broken, too. The pastors may feel helpless. The elders and deacons may find themselves disagreeing on how to turn things around. Some may grasp at more power while others choose to leave or start their own church.

An interesting ministry model and leadership dynamic that I discovered from my study of Nehemiah is that he mastered the skill and insight of knowing to whom he should share and delegate ministerial responsibilities, as well as how and when to do this. At this critical juncture, giving power to the wrong people can be disastrous for you and for the church.

For instance, in Nehemiah chapters 8 and 9, Nehemiah intentionally stepped aside, passing the ministerial leadership baton to Ezra the scribe and the Levite priests. Doing this allowed them to instruct the people in the laws and statutes of God. It was now their responsibility to rebuild the people spiritually by instructing them how to live for and honor the same Yahweh-God that had brought their forefathers out of Egyptian captivity.

Gaebelein suggests that Ezra had desired to lead the people in the ways of the Lord for some time, but the state of the city and the despair of the people prevented him from sharing his good news.[15] Once Nehemiah relieved Jerusalem of its physical burden, Ezra could do what he did best—preach, teach, and be a spiritual leader.

It is imperative that we know our gifts and limitations. For instance, most managers are awesome at what they do, but left alone, they make poor pastors. Why? Because they are very good at managing what is placed under their control, but seldom are they willing to take risk and step out in faith.

As a result, they will manage a church to a gradual death. So every manager needs a visionary pastor and every pastor need a good manager, just like Nehemiah and Ezra. So, if you are a visionary pastor, find a good manager. Not only will they bring balance and keep you between heaven and earth as you lead your congregation but also they will hold you accountable and create transparency and a high level of trust within and without the church.

In the same way, as you are in the process of rebuilding a broken-down church or ministry, you may find yourself coming alongside former leaders or even laypeople in the church who have never been able to fulfill their God-given callings to serve, due to previous dysfunctions and infighting within the body.

You may also come across leaders or self-appointed leaders who simply are not fit for their roles. Knowing how to navigate these delicate relationships will take much prayer, fasting, and reliance upon God. It will also help to reference these restoration principles as you prayerfully consider how to find ways to encourage those sitting on the sidelines to step into service while you carefully approach those currently in leadership roles that are not suited for them.

Rebuilding Principle #5
Protect the Weak and Vulnerable from Extortionists

Now the men and their wives raised a great outcry against

their fellow Jews. Some were saying, "We and our sons and daughters are numerous; in order for us to eat and stay alive, we must get grain."

Others were saying, "We are mortgaging our fields, our vineyards and our homes to get grain during the famine."

Still others were saying, "We have had to borrow money to pay the king's tax on our fields and vineyards. Although we are of the same flesh and blood as our fellow Jews and though our children are as good as theirs, yet we have to subject our sons and daughters to slavery. Some of our daughters have already been enslaved, but we are powerless, because our fields and our vineyards belong to others."

—Nehemiah 5:1–5

This passage in Nehemiah chapter 5 is an example of how people in power can take advantage of people who are weak, broken, and in need. Just as this was a threat and problem for the Jews, it's also a major concern in churches today. While many church leaders rise up with the best of intentions, there are some whose goals are to seek power, money, and success—and they plan to use a church body or a ministry to get there. They create what Plueddemann calls, "power distances" in the church.[16]

This is unbiblical and unChristlike, and if left unchecked will breed a power-hungry, toxic culture in the church. This will ultimately result in the creation of factions and friction instead of synergy and unity in the body. Praying for wisdom and being aware that there may be someone in your church or ministry who does not have the best intentions at heart is an important part of building your ministry teams and selecting people for service.

Rebuilding Principle #6:
Cultivate and Maintain an Attitude of Joy

Ezra praised the LORD, the great God; and all the people lifted their hands and responded, "Amen! Amen!" Then they bowed down and worshiped the LORD with their faces to the ground.
—Nehemiah 8:6

It's often said that great leaders lead by example, and Nehemiah and Ezra proved this. They could have been frustrated. They could have been angry. After all, Ezra had spent years in Jerusalem, dealing with the aftermath of a destroyed city wall and a dejected, demoralized and vulnerable people. Nehemiah could have easily been burdened and overwhelmed by the great task that he had undertaken. Yet both chose a stance of worship and praise God regularly.

Sometimes your posture as a leader can either elevate, aggravate or stagnate your followers. Aaron and Hur knew the secret to posture power, which is why they insisted on elevating Moses' hand in a worshipping posture when he could not do it himself (Exodus 17:12).

In Nehemiah 8:6, Ezra called the people to praise God. And in 8:10, Nehemiah said that "the joy of the LORD is your strength." The prophet Hosea explained how spiritual leaders can impact the lives of their followers, by influencing them, and the fault falls to both (Hosea 4:9).

These messages came at a time when the people had just heard the word of the Lord spoken for the first time in many years. They had responded with grief as they thought about all the ways they had fallen short of God's intention for them and their city. They felt the enormity of the changes that were before them—they knew they would never be right with God unless they turned their city around.

And yet Ezra and Nehemiah called the people to public worship and joy. Sometimes when we look around us, conditions may never be perfect or conducive to praise. But that's the time to make an altar right where you are and offer yourself as a living sacrifice and a sweet smelling savor to the Lord. I have come to realize the more challenging my circumstances are, the more pure my praise and worship becomes. The fires we go through purify and fortify our faith, and only a faith that is tested can be trusted.

As leaders in broken or dying ministries, we will encounter many individuals who are grieving, bitter, confused, or angry. In such situations it may be tempting to join them in their gloom, especially if you've been a long-time member of the church or ministry you're working to rebuild.

This is why it is so vital to continually and actively seek direction from the Holy Spirit throughout the process and surround yourself with other spiritual leaders who will speak words of hope and joy into your life. When you are filled with the joy of the Lord, you are in turn able to spread that joy to the members of your congregation.

At our church I call it "getting and keeping your spiritual equilibrium." Nehemiah and Ezra intentionally shifted the culture from having a mind to worry to having "a mind to work" (Nehemiah 4:6). Then they promoted and modeled the principles of joy and happiness in the midst of challenges by cultivating a new mindset of genuine encouragement.

The results were a revived, recalibrated, empowered, and motivated people. Former generations could not have rebuilt the walls of Jerusalem in over one hundred years. But with this new mindset, new leadership, and new strategy, they got it done in fifty-two days. A lazy, unmotivated, spiritually apathetic mindset will hold your future hostage and rob you of God's best for your life.

Change Worth Keeping

The greatest part of the church restoration process is watching as the community and leaders experience a complete transformation as the Word of God takes root in their lives and new habits and mindsets set in. You'll soon find that this life-change is ongoing. You must be intentional to cultivate a culture of perpetual spiritual formation.

As you implement an attitude of joy and carefully groom and disciple people for leadership and ministry, you'll realize that the need for rebuilding and restoration doesn't end once the church is fully restored. You may just have clearer lenses to see the next level and a better team to travel with you.

Today we have ongoing leadership development training for those who desire to be leaders or who would like to be appointed to any of our boards and leadership teams. We have a healthy vetting process, and we strive to maintain an attitude of joy and synergy—no matter how difficult the situation.

This model has become such an important aspect of what we do that I couldn't imagine the church without it. We need to help our people find their strengths and spiritual giftedness. We need to guide them if they're headed toward leadership, and we need to model a positive, healthy outlook to the congregation and community as a whole.

The thought of uprooting the leadership hierarchy and "starting fresh" in your church or ministry may seem daunting. And waking up with a positive attitude, going up against adversity with joy in your heart may also seem like a pipe dream.

But just as God made a way for Nehemiah and Ezra, he will make a way for you and for the people you're trying to help. He wants this for you. He knows how important it is. And He's going to do everything He can to help get you there.

WORKBOOK

Chapter Four Questions

Question: Who are some leaders or potential leaders in the church who have not been able to minister effectively with their gifts because of their brokenness? How can you come alongside and encourage them to fulfill their God-given callings and reach their full potential?

_____

_____

_____

_____

_____

_____

_____

_____

_____

Question: Who are some people in leadership positions who need to be removed or redirected in order to make peace and create unity in the church body?

_____

_____

_____

_____

_____

_____

_____

_____

_____

Action: Re-examine your list above—people who may need to be removed from or redirected in their service— with the following evaluation:

1. What is the concern with each person?

2. Is there a different place of service where they can be more effective?

3. Has this person caused division and broken trust, and if so, are they willing to confess and make things right?

4. Are there leaders who have so damaged the church that they need to be asked to leave or to step down from all leadership positions?

5. Are there outside influences of "famous" Christian teachers whose teaching is causing confusion or conflict in the church? How can their influence be removed?

6. Is your church equipped with a council of spiritually mature leaders that can offer wise council to ineffective leaders in an effort to rebuild and recalibrate them?

Spend focused time in prayer about the best way to approach each of these situations and persons so as to optimize healing and minimize conflict and division.

Question: What is the attitude around the church? Are people happy and excited to be there, or are they fearful and anxious about what's going to happen next?

_____

_____

_____

_____

_____

_____

_____

_____

_____

_____

Question: How can you model joy to the congregation? How will you offer sincere encouragement to the grieving and loving exhortation to the angry?

_____

_____

_____

_____

_____

_____

_____

_____

_____

Question: What sort of fellowship (optimally, something outside of the regular church services) could help to build relationships and restore a sense of family and joy?

_____

_____

_____

_____

_____

_____

_____

_____

_____

_____

Action: Work with a trusted team of church leaders, or if necessary, a team from outside of the broken ministry to develop a sound vetting process for choosing lay and staff church leadership. Create written guidelines for each ministry position in the church, keeping your qualifications simple, straightforward, and biblical.

Guide the congregation in discovering their spiritual gifts and personality strengths. There are many excellent evaluation tools available for this purpose. Let it be a time of joy as you realize God's unique plan and purpose for each member and for the body as a whole.

Chapter Four Notes

_____

_____

_____

_____

_____

_____

_____

_____

_____

_____

_____

_____

_____

_____

_____

_____

_____

_____

_____

_____

_____

CHAPTER FIVE

Rebuilding Broken People

Now the city was large and spacious, but there were few people in it, and the houses had not yet been rebuilt. So my God put it into my heart to assemble the nobles, the officials and the common people for registration by families. I found the genealogical record of those who had been the first to return.

—Nehemiah 7:4–5

Bible scholar John Barach observes that the book of Nehemiah can be divided into two sections. While the first half of the book focuses on the rebuilding of the city and city walls itself, the second half describes a "re-instruction of the people."[17] Here's how it breaks down in the text.

In Nehemiah chapters 7 through 10, dynamic leadership principles for addressing spiritual and social problems are carefully observed. In chapter seven Nehemiah intentionally took a census of the remaining Jewish exiles (Nehemiah 7:4–73), then he assigned his brother Hanani to be governor of Jerusalem, and also appointed a man by the name of Hananiah to oversee the remaining work and protection of the city (Nehemiah 7:1–3). Then in chapter eight Ezra communicated the Book of the Law to the people, getting the Levites to explain the meaning of the message to the people (Nehemiah 8:1–12). After the people heard and understood the Word of the Law, they responded with tears, confession of their sins, and public worship (Nehemiah 9:1–38).

Finally in chapter 10, the people and their families made written promises to faithfully serve the God of Abraham, Isaac and Jacob. They brought promissory documents to be signed by Nehemiah, the priests, the Levites, the political leaders, the gate keepers, the singers, and others (Nehemiah 10:1–28). From this point on, every effort was made to bring people into the city and restore their relationships with the Lord.

This shift in focus from social appointments to spiritual matters resulted in a spiritual reform in Jerusalem. It ended up being temporary and short-lived, but it was spiritual reform, nonetheless.

A spiritual reform is one of the greatest goals for any broken church or ministry. As Nehemiah shows, spiritual reform happens when a number of factors are carefully considered and addressed.

Rebuilding Principle #7
Understand the Culture of the People to Whom You're Ministering

You might not be able to call for a census of our respective cities and towns like Nehemiah did, but you do have access to state and federal resources that can give a basic overview of the various people groups and socio-economics surrounding your church. You can compare this against the families and individuals who form your congregation, getting a most complete picture of the demographics, needs, and backgrounds of those within your city and sanctuary.

While evaluating the struggling churches in south Florida, I discovered a few things that shed some light on what was contributing to the brokenness of the people sitting in the pews. In my research, I discovered that some of the most critical social issues and major concerns affecting the people and churches in the city of Lauderhill are HIV/AIDS, poverty, and crime.

According to the Florida Department of Health and Broward County Health Department's 2012 census, Broward county, where Lauderhill is annexed, "is the second highest populated HIV/AIDS County in the United States." I also learned that over seventeen percent of the population live under the poverty level. Other critical issues include high teenage pregnancy, fatherlessness, single parenting, illegal immigrants, and dependent elderly parents.[18]

When I considered the physical position of my church, I found major hospitals, schools, colleges, the city hall, police headquarters, pawn shop, malls, and the YMCA close by. Furthermore, Lauderhill is about ten miles from Las Olas, one of the most popular vacation destinations in Fort Lauderdale.

Yet despite the appearance of wealth surrounding our church building, my congregation itself came from homes that struggled financially.

This information proved invaluable. Like Nehemiah, who stated that his objective was to "promote the welfare of the Israelites" (Nehemiah 2:10), I too was burdened for the people and churches in south Florida. After reading these statistics and evaluating the spiritual and social conditions of this community, I proposed a two-part action plan for rebuilding the church's approach.

First, foster a spiritual transformation from the inside the church, beginning with the leadership.

Second, engage with the community in social reformation outside church walls.

By understanding how best to serve the people in my city and my church, I was able to work with others to raise up programs and services that spoke directly to their biggest needs. Everything, from the outreach programs we enacted to the morning worship service time, was tailored to be a fit for the people of Lauderhill and the surrounding area.

Rebuilding Principle #8:
Engage the Community and Meet Needs

In May 2014, our church partnered with the Lauderhill YMCA; Lauderhill Middle School; the International School of Health, Beauty and Technology; several local businesses and healthcare organizations; and grocery stores to host a "Rock the Block" event. This event was a product of the demographic information that we had researched months prior.

From "Rock the Block" to "Rock the City." These community programs provided free groceries, meals, and social services to our community. In addition, we teamed up with some nonprofit organizations like Operation Compassion, Farm Share, Feed South Florida, Feeding America, Publix supermarkets, Bridging the Gap, EHC, SNAP, Church of God Chaplains Commission, and various church members and friends to distribute over 25,000 pounds of food to Lauderhill and other neighboring communities.

Five thousand blankets were also donated by Jim Campbell, Director for the Homeless Coalition of America. Operation Compassion, a disaster relief ministry of the Church of God donated over seventeen hundred English and Spanish Bibles, and they sent a team of eleven volunteers to help with the distribution of these items. The Church of God Chaplains Commission sent a representative to help us serve food and the gospel through acts of kindness to the people of the Lauderhill community.

This was a very successful event that truly demonstrated the love of God and the mission of the body of Christ. It is a prime example of what it means to engage with your community and be a church that genuinely C.A.R.E.S, with an incarnational leadership that demonstrates the love of God through:

1. Connecting people to Christ,
2. Affirming them in their faith,
3. Resourcing them to reach their full potential, and
4. Educating them to be agents of positive change in order to
5. Serve effectively in the Kingdom of God.

You, too, can put together a church strategy and event that is based on the real-life needs and realities of the people within your community. If homelessness is a problem, you can open a soup kitchen or team up with a local mission. If single parenting is prevalent, you can launch a childcare ministry or a diapers-and-clothing pantry.

If your area is heavily affluent, you can find ways to reach businesspeople. This may entail offering Bible studies or opening your church up as a place where entrepreneurs can work during the day and managers can bring their teams for an afternoon offsite breakout.

Once you know the people you're serving, the ideas for reaching and engaging them will be abundant—I guarantee it. Remember, your goal is never to impress the people your community, only to impact the people in your community. When your church reaches this stage, you no longer pastor your local church, you pastor the community where God has placed your church.

Doing, Growing, and Flowing

Outreach is one of those things that we all know we should be doing, yet it can be intimidating. You may feel like a fish out of water as you try to extend an invitation to folks who may look nothing like you. But the benefits go well beyond knowing that you're helping to make others' lives better.

I saw this firsthand during our Rock the Block outreach. Church members who had been divided, bitter, and unforgiving toward one another were working together joyfully as they served our community!

It was one of the most pleasant and astonishing realities to behold. Just eleven months prior, these people had been broken, divided, and hostile. This is evidence of the importance of coming together as a church and giving back.

It also shows that the Creator of the world can and does build and rebuild his church in ways unknown to man. I was reminded of the words of the Lord recorded by Isaiah: "'For my thoughts are not your thoughts, neither are your ways my ways,' declares the LORD" (Isaiah 55:8).

I am convinced that God used this event to mobilize His people around a common purpose, to reestablish unity, and to restore brotherly love within the congregation *before* bringing so many to saving faith in Christ and adding them to his church.

In the same way, Nehemiah not only rallied the people within the broken-down walls of Jerusalem to get involved and help rebuild, but he also got the heathen King Artaxerxes and Queen to help fund the completion of the rebuilding project (Nehemiah 2:1–8). How mysteriously God works!

In the year following the Rock the Block community outreach, the church's membership grew about twenty-five percent. Fifty-three new lay leaders were trained, strengthening our church ministries, and eighty newly ordained disciples began serving and assisting in our food bank, food pantry, and care ministries. In addition, several leadership boards and committees were appointed and are still active to this day.

The church's missions and outreach programs are presently assisting over two thousand people per month, and we've also begun networking with our hospitals and community health centers to offer a much-needed healthcare strategy to the underprivileged and less fortunate in our community, especially our seniors.

I believe this is just the beginning. The more we step out and engage the community, meeting their needs, the more doors God opens. The more our church grows. And the more passionate we become about our Lord, our faith, and our calling.

For you, it starts with a spiritual transformation within your church.

Up to this point, most of this book has been about how to quiet your heart and lead your people toward a deeper relationship with God. It's the single most important thing you can do as you keep in step with the Holy Spirit to rebuild and restore your church or ministry.

But once that heart position is in place—once God has a hold of your congregation—then it's time to engage. Research your community, develop a plan, and then put it into action. Leave it to God to do the rest. Remember it's a co-mission not a solo mission. God is committed to building His kingdom and also to those involved.

WORKBOOK

Chapter Five Questions

Question: Have you ever witnessed or been a part of a spiritual revival or reform? What factors typically accompany a corporate movement of God? How can you help put your church/ministry in a position to be ready for spiritual reformation?

_____

_____

_____

_____

_____

_____

_____

_____

_____

_____

_____

Question: Describe the demographics of the people within your church (e.g., white collar/blue collar, education level, family size and structure, economic conditions, government dependence or independence, typical spiritual heritage, and background).

_____

_____

_____

_____

_____

_____

_____

_____

_____

Question: Next, describe the environment around your church, including an assessment of the same factors above. Is your church similar to or very different from the community in which it resides?

_____

_____

_____

_____

_____

_____

_____

_____

_____

_____

_____

Question: What would you identify as five key tangible needs in your immediate community? How could your church be involved in meeting one or more of these needs? Would a one-time event or an ongoing program be most feasible for your congregation?

_____

_____

_____

_____

_____

_____

_____

_____

_____

_____

_____

Question: What businesses, government entities, or local nonprofits could come alongside to help? Who in the church already has a heart for this type of outreach? Who already has connections to potentially partnering community resources?

_____

_____

_____

_____

_____

_____

_____

_____

_____

_____

Action: Look at the answers to the questions above. What community need(s) is your church strategically and providentially poised to meet?

It is important that this outreach initiative be a time of unifying the church. How will this be a team effort, and not a directive from you? Pray about how and when you will present it to the congregation.

Write out a proposal for the ministry initiative and discuss it with the church leadership.

_____

_____

_____

_____

_____

_____

_____

_____

_____

_____

_____

Chapter Five Notes

_____

_____

_____

_____

_____

_____

_____

_____

_____

_____

_____

_____

_____

_____

_____

_____

_____

_____

_____

_____

CONCLUSION

The Rebuilt Church

In His book, *Twelve Sermons on Nehemiah*, John Barach used a simple, yet profound exegetical and hermeneutical approach in extracting four dynamic principles from the fourth chapter of Nehemiah. After prayer and fasting, Nehemiah first instructed the people to remove the rubble. Second, he told them to restore their fellowship with God. Third, Nehemiah reminded them to resist the enemy. Finally, he commanded them, to rely on God.[19]

I consider the fourth chapter of Nehemiah to be pivotal. There is so much for church leaders to glean. I'd like to conclude this book by using Barach's principles as the framework for my own four-step action plan for rearing and rebuilding broken churches. I believe that these four points can be adopted by any pastor or lay leader who may be called to rebuild broken churches and communities of faith.

In other words, if you come away from reading this book with one stand-out principle or method, this should be it.

Step 1: Remove the Rubble

You can't build a new church on a pile of ruin (Nehemiah 4:10). It won't stand. To rebuild a physical church building, we must first clear out the rubble.

The same principle applies to our spiritual lives and pastoral ministry.

Our sins and the sins of the church must be addressed and dealt with before sustainable spiritual rebuilding can take place. We cannot ignore a little sin here and there— be it unforgiveness, pride, a little white lie, a little gossip, lust, prejudice, hatred—and expect to have strong faith and a productive Christian life.

Furthermore, we cannot expect success when we are doing little or nothing to seek the Lord in prayer, worship, and study. Without the Lord, it is impossible to remove the debris, rubble, rubbish, and junk from our lives. The only way we can clear the land and rebuild again is to give God free access to cultivate our hearts like His.

Therefore, in order to move out of the rubble heaps of wreck and ruin and into the mission field of God's plan for His church, it is necessary to teach our congregation the spiritual disciplines of prayer, fasting, stewardship, and God's plan for a godly family. It is also imperative that we teach our leaders as we model the "fruit of the Spirit" (Galatians 5:22–23) in our everyday lives—not just when we're standing at the pulpit.

These spiritual characteristics of love, joy peace, forbearance, kindness, goodness, faithfulness, gentleness, and self-control (Galatians 5:22–23) must be modeled by the entire leadership team in order for there to be spiritual cohesiveness and perpetual synergy in the church as it moves forward.

To recap:

1. Clear out the rubble (sin, etc.).
2. Establish spiritual disciplines (such as prayer, fasting, Bible study, worship, etc.).
3. Live out the fruit of the Spirit.

When enacted on a personal level, these three steps will clear the rubble from your life. When enacted on a corporate level, these three steps will make the way for a major church turnaround.

Step 2: Restore Fellowship with God and People

Nehemiah understood the awesome value of fellowship with God through a consistent prayer life, which he modeled throughout the book of Nehemiah (Nehemiah 1:5–11; 5:19; 6:14; 13:14, 22, 29, 31). Even when the people felt discouraged, disillusioned, and overwhelmed, Nehemiah was quick to say, "Remember the Lord, who is great and awesome" (Nehemiah 4:14).

Jehoshaphat, a former king of Judah, made a similar example of faith through prayer by stating before the disheartened and scared Jews, "For we have no power to face this vast army that is attacking us. We do not know what to do, but our eyes are on you" (2 Chronicles 20:12).

I have found that a healthy relationship and fellowship with God and with people is one of the most important overarching themes of the Bible. Therefore, I have personally developed a ministry model to help our church grow closer to God and each other in fellowship and communion. My ministry model is called FEAST that stands for Families Eating and Studying Together. The main objective of FEAST is to repair and rebuild the families in my church and the surrounding communities by coaching them into stronger and healthier relationships.

FEAST is intentionally designed to help meet the needs of struggling families during the busy mid-week. For instance, every Wednesday evening our church provides a hot dinner for families in need. Following dinner, our volunteer teachers assist elementary and middle school children with their homework, while their parents, older siblings, and other family members are encouraged to attend a small group Bible study. We also provide a nursery for babies.

My objective is simple: our church exists to help busy, struggling families and single parents who need assistance, community, and who want to experience a better life. The church exists to demonstrate that "better life" to the people in their neighborhoods and communities through loving acts of kindness as Jesus commanded when he described the scene of the final judgment in Matthew 25:31–40.

I utilized this same ministry with success over a period of twelve years during my time serving as a senior pastor in Chicago. I have found it to be beneficial for restoring the church as well as restoring the outside community. It adds new life to traditional and struggling mid-week services in churches, especially in an urban context. Another great benefit of FEAST is that it mobilizes the membership of the local church into active in-reach and outreach ministries, coupled with consistent community service.

Done correctly, such a program can reestablish order and structure among leaders, create synergy among members, build momentum for the church to move forward, and close the revolving door of membership retention and ongoing church growth.

Step 3: Resist the Enemy

In this third principle, Nehemiah highlighted the strategy for warfare and how to deal with unrelenting opposition. He nuanced in Nehemiah 4:16–18, "From that day on, half of my men did the work, while the other half were equipped with spears, shields, bows and armor. The officers posted themselves behind all the people of Judah who were building the wall. Those who carried materials did their work with one hand and held a weapon in the other, and each of the builders wore his sword at his side as he worked."

Interestingly, this is a profound principle that every believer in the church of Jesus Christ should know. I concur with author John Barach, who suggests that "the sword and the trowel should always go together and that building should be more important than battling."[20] It is my opinion that the enemy of the church of Jesus Christ is working overtime to distract God's people from doing the work of God in many places in the earth. By keeping God's people stuck in battle mode, the enemy hopes to wear us down, diverting us from building and advancing God's kingdom.

After I arrived at the church in south Florida and began to rebuild the infrastructure of the church, there were several internal and external battles that had to be dealt with immediately. These battles threatened to completely steal my focus and hijack my vision.

Nevertheless, I did not allow these relational, spiritual, and financial challenges to distract or hinder the work and mission that was in my heart. Instead, I used them as a catalyst to mobilize the congregation in unrelenting prayer, fasting, and fundraising. I intentionally shifted the ringleaders of these power-struggle groups from fighting *with* each other to fighting *for* each other. Some even turned on me. That's how quickly the winds can change in a toxic ministry context, so you must be always on your guard and keep your spiritual armor on, and stand firm.

As the apostle Paul reminded the believers in Ephesus, "For our struggle is not against flesh and blood, but against the rulers, against the authorities, against the powers of this dark world and against the spiritual forces of evil in the heavenly realms" (Ephesians 6:12). It was my intention to keep the purpose and mission of the church before the people, as Jesus did before his disciples in Caesarea Philippi.

By using Peter as an example, Jesus made it crystal clear to his disciples when he declared, "On this rock I will build my church, and the gates of Hades [hell] will not overcome it" (Matthew 16:18). Christ, the head of the Church, also affirmed that the enemy only comes to "steal and kill and destroy" (John 10:10).

Scripture clearly instructs us to resist the Devil so he will flee from us (James 4:7). And Peter also referred to the Devil as the "adversary" whom we must resist firmly in the faith (1 Peter 5:8–9 NKJV). Hence, because we are in a spiritual battle, we are taught from Scripture that in order to resist the Devil, we must first submit to Christ (Ephesians 6:10–20; Romans 6:17–23; James 4:7).

Think about it: if the enemy can get believers, churches, and denominations to fight against one another, as he was trying to do at this church in south Florida, then as a result the work of God would be hindered, people would continue to leave the church frustrated and confused, and unbelievers would remain lost in their sin—all because the enemy of the church has the people of God too busy battling each other instead of building and advancing the Kingdom of God.

There is a lot of emphasis on "spiritual warfare" in our evangelical and Pentecostal churches today, but let us not forget Jesus' commands regarding global evangelization as outlined in the great commission recorded in Matthew 28:18–20:

All authority in heaven and on earth has been given to me. Therefore go and make disciples of all nations, baptizing them in the name of the Father and of the Son and of the

Holy Spirit, and teaching them to obey everything I have commanded you. And surely I am with you always, to the very end of the age.

What Jesus emphasized there is what I am hoping to achieve as pastor of the church in Lauderhill, Florida, and it's what you should be striving for in your own church or ministry. By actively acting out and sharing our faith, we can work against the enemy's advances.

Step 4: Rely on God

The most profound spiritual principle and common denominator that I have discovered in Nehemiah's personality and leadership style has to be this: Nehemiah totally relied on God from beginning to the end of his assignment. He was intentional about keeping God at the center of everything he did before the people, and as a result, his life project of rebuilding the wall and restoring the city was not about Nehemiah but about the goodness and favor of God toward His covenant people Israel.

This is the spirit of *The Rebuilder* that I hope and pray would be imparted to everyone reading this book. Whatever has been broken down in your life can be rebuilt in the Spirit and name of The Rebuilder, Jesus Christ. Jesus affirmed that He is the greatest rebuilder of all times by declaring, "Destroy this temple and in three days I will raise it up again," and "No one takes it from me, but I lay it down of my own accord. *I have authority to lay it down and authority to take it up again.* This command I received from my Father" (John 2:19; 10:18, emphasis added).

Like Nehemiah, we must intentionally keep God at the center and fulcrum of every endeavor of our personal life and ministry. I am convinced and persuaded that the successful turnaround of this church in south Florida is attributed to a total reliance on the power and plan of the Holy Spirit. It is only because of the grace of God and total reliance on Him that we have been able to turn this church around spiritually and financially. No secular methods could work. The church of the living God is a spiritual body, and will only be rebuilt by spiritual methods. I have noticed many over the years trying to recalibrate their church with secular methods and after a few years they are burned out and frustrated. My friends, just be patient and rely on the sovereignty of God's perfect timing. He will guide you safely through every impossible door.

People in our community are coming to Christ, being baptized, and becoming active members of our congregation. Our evangelism and community outreach mission has grown from feeding and caring for a few hundred people in and around Lauderhill to caring for over two thousand persons per month.

We saw miraculous financial debt cancellation, the repaving of the parking lot, abundant remodeling, significant upgrades to the media department, and a refreshing of the landscaping. As I write this chapter, we are getting ready to build a fence to secure the entire property, and all of these projects are being done debt-free.

But the greatest rebuilding is not seen in the brick and mortar, but in the healing of broken relationships, and the growth of our members spiritually and numerically can only be described in the infallible words of the apostle Paul to the Saints in Rome, "If God is for us, who can be against us?" (Romans 8:31).

Therefore, like Nehemiah, I am convinced and am persuaded that when we totally rely on God and also teach our congregation to put their trust and confidence in the Lord, we will have good success as we rebuild the people and house of the Lord.

What This Means for You

You may have come to the end of this book feeling overwhelmed. You have suspected that you, your family, church, business or ministry was broken, and you're beginning to feel a bit of brokenness yourself. How will you be able to turn the congregation to the Lord, balance the budget, reach out to the community, build up the right leadership staff, and have the hard conversations that need to be had?

On your own, this task is monumental and impossible. But God makes a way. Seek Him. Pray. Fast. Follow the Spirit's promptings in your heart. It all starts with you having a posture of surrender and humility. From there, others will be impacted. They will want change. They will see the brokenness, and as they seek and follow God, they will find ways to help. Don't spend another moment worrying about tomorrow. Focus your attention on the calling of God that is on your life and the assignment that you were created for. God will always bring the right people and resources into your life when you remain faithful to the assignment he has entrusted to you. Challenges will come, but so will positive changes. Enemies may arise, but so are prayer warriors. Pressure may be unbearable at times, but God will never give you more than you can handle. Worry and uncertainty may invade your heart and ministry, but that's God's opportunity to unleash His divine prosperity, unstoppable power and uncommon favor in your life, family and ministry. Remember the Rebuilder's song, "The Joy of the Lord Is My Strength."

It's a group effort, but it always starts with one. You are the one that God will use to rebuild broken things. Prepare your heart. Move forward in faith. It's time to rekindle your vision, regain your focus, release your faith, revive your family, restore your finances, rebuild your ministry, repent of your sins and the sins of your community, resurrect your dreams, recalibrate your culture, remove unrighteousness of your life, and become a refreshing spring for those around you.

Use this book as a reference guide to the eight rebuilding principles. Then, go out and do God's work. The Spirit of the One that specializes in rebuilding nations and lives in you and wants to use you to rebuild the broken lives of others and affirmed his infallible Word by declaring through the prophet in Isaiah, "Your people will rebuild the ancient ruins and will raise up the age-old foundations; you will be called Repairer of Broken Walls, Restorer of Streets with Dwellings" (Isaiah 58:12).

WORKBOOK

Conclusion Questions

Question: What sin and distractions (Hebrews 12:1) are creating rubble in your own life? In your congregation? How will you call the church to repentance?

_____

_____

_____

_____

_____

_____

_____

_____

Question: What spiritual disciplines have you neglected personally? Which ones have been neglected corporately? How will you hold each other accountable to be faithful in these disciplines?

_____

_____

_____

_____

_____

_____

_____

_____

_____

Question: Is your own life characterized by the fruit of the Spirit? Do these qualities describe your church as a whole? Which ones need shoring up, and how will you follow the Holy Spirit in obedience so that He can build them into your lives?

_____

_____

_____

_____

_____

_____

_____

_____

_____

_____

Question: What specific programs and ministries of your church help people to grow in closer fellowship to God and each other?

_____

_____

_____

_____

_____

_____

_____

_____

_____

_____

Question: In what ways are you or can you encourage authentic relationships and intentional discipleship?

_____

_____

_____

_____

_____

_____

_____

_____

_____

_____

Question: In what ways is your church engaged in "spiritual warfare"? Are the battle lines drawn against one another? What are the "camps" within the church who seek to destroy one another? How can the focus be shifted from winning and being right to submitting to Christ and serving each other and the community in love?

_____

_____

_____

_____

_____

_____

_____

_____

_____

_____

_____

Question: What are some practical ways to shift the focus from external, temporal, or preference issues to the much greater calling of the Great Commission?

_____

_____

_____

_____

_____

_____

_____

_____

_____

Question: Are you more focused on church growth experts and strategies or on the wisdom of God? Do you spend more energy in prayer or in seeking man's advice for the church rebuilding that you face? If everyone in your church relied on God to the same extent that you do, would you be a church that is totally dependent on Him?

_____

_____

_____

_____

_____

_____

_____

_____

_____

_____

_____

_____

Action: What does it mean to be broken before God? Do a scriptural study on this attitude of spiritual brokenness. How does it ultimately lead to divine healing and wholeness? Are you broken or willing to be broken before God for the sake of His church's rebuilding, restoration, revival, and the advancement of His kingdom?

_____

_____

_____

_____

_____

_____

_____

_____

_____

Conclusion Notes

_____

_____

_____

_____

_____

_____

_____

_____

_____

_____

_____

_____

_____

_____

_____

_____

_____

_____

_____

_____

APPENDIX

The Rebuilder's Toolbox

The wall was completed in fifty and two days.
—Nehemiah 6:15

Every builder needs a toolbox to effectively complete their assigned project. I was once told by professional builders that a builder is only as good as the tools he or she possesses.

The Rebuilder's Toolbox contains fifty-two necessary scriptures to help you rebuild whatever is broken in your faith, family, finances, and ministry. Remember, rebuilding is not an overnight parade; it's a prayerful and careful journey. So, master one principle per week for fifty-two weeks, believing God for the impossible.

The Rebuilder's Toolbox

Tool #1. The Trowel of Truth: "The day for building your walls will come, the day for extending your boundaries" (Micah 7:11).

Tool #2. The Drill of Discipline: "Then the king commanded, and they quarried great stones, costly stones, to lay the foundation of the house with cut stones" (1 Kings 5:17).

Tool # 3. The Ax of Faith: "'Go up to the mountains, bring wood and rebuild the temple, that I may be pleased with it and be glorified,' says the LORD" (Haggai 1:8).

Tool #4. The Pliers of Persistence: "After this I will return and rebuild David's fallen tent. Its ruins I will rebuild, and I will restore it" (Acts 15:16).

Tool #5. The Plow of Patience: "They will rebuild the ruined cities and live in them. They will plant vineyards and drink their wine; they will make gardens and eat their fruit" (Amos 9:14).

Tool #6. The Ratchet of Restoration: "In that day I will restore David's fallen shelter. I will repair its broken walls and restore its ruins, and will rebuild it as it used to be" (Amos 9:11).

Tool #7. The Ladder of Love: "I will bring Judah and Israel back from captivity and will rebuild" (Jeremiah 33:7).

Tool #8. The Claw Hammer of Hope: "I am able to destroy the temple of God and rebuild it in three days" (Matthew 26:61).

Tool #9. The Allen Keys of Divine Alignment: "The Fountain Gate was repaired by Shallun son of Kol-Hozeh, ruler of the district of Mizpah. He rebuilt it, roofing it over and aligned its doors and bolts and bars in place" (Nehemiah 3:15).

Tool #10. The Stud Finder of Team Support: "Then Zerubbabel son of Shealtiel and Joshua son of Jozadak set to work to rebuild the house of God in Jerusalem. And the prophets of God were with them, supporting them" (Ezra 5:2).

Tool #11. The Rope of Reliance: "Know and understand this: From the time the word goes out to restore and rebuild Jerusalem until the Anointed One, the ruler, comes, there will be seven 'sevens,' and sixty-two 'sevens.' It will be rebuilt with streets and a trench, but in times of trouble" (Daniel 9:25).

Tool #12. The Plunger of Promise: "They will rebuild the ancient ruins and restore the places long devastated; they will renew the ruined cities that have been devastated for generations" (Isaiah 61:4).

Tool #13. The Nails of Organizational Stability: "Do not interfere with the work on this temple of God. Let the governor of the Jews and the Jewish elders rebuild this house of God on its site" (Ezra 6:7).

Tool #14. The Bolts and Nuts of Delegated Authority: "We questioned the elders and asked them, 'Who authorized you to rebuild this temple and to finish it?'" (Ezra 5:9).

Tool #15. The Rivets of Redemption: "You will rebuild those houses left in ruins for years; you will be known as a builder and repairer of city walls and streets" (Isaiah 58:12 CEV).

Tool #16. The Crowbar of Courage: "The bricks have fallen down, but we will rebuild with dressed stone; the fig trees have been felled, but we will replace them with cedars" (Isaiah 9:10).

Tool #17. The Caliper of Favor: "Foreigners will rebuild your walls, and their kings will serve you. Though in anger I struck you, in favor I will show you compassion" (Isaiah 60:10).

Tool #18. The Duct Tape of Unity: "So built we the walls, for the people had a mind to work" (Nehemiah 4:6).

Tool #19. The Rake of Resilience: "Now issue an order to these men to stop work, so that this city will not be rebuilt until I so order" (Ezra 4:21).

Tool #20. The Tape Measure of Mercy: "Then the nations around you that remain will know that I the LORD have rebuilt what was destroyed and have replanted what was desolate. I the LORD have spoken, and I will do it" (Ezekiel 36:36).

Tool #21. The Plumb-line of Prophecy: "The day is coming," says the LORD, "when all Jerusalem will be rebuilt for me, from the Tower of Hananel to the Corner Gate" (Jeremiah 31:38 NLT).

Tool #22. The Pencil of Peace: "Solomon rebuilt the villages that Hiram had given him, and settled the Israelites in them" (2 Chronicles 8:2).

Tool #23. The Sledgehammer of Wisdom and Knowledge: "I will certainly give you the wisdom and knowledge you requested. But I will also give you wealth, riches, and fame such as no other king has had before you or will ever have in the future!" (2 Chronicles 1:12 NLT).

Tool #24. The Gloves of Completion: "The hands of Zerubbabel have laid the foundation of this temple; his hands will also complete it. Then you will know that the LORD Almighty has sent me to you" (Zechariah 4:6).

Tool #25. The Spirit Level of Leadership: "After the wall had been rebuilt and I had set the doors in place, the gatekeepers, the musicians and the Levites were appointed" (Nehemiah 7:1).

Tool #26. The Flashlight of Discernment: "When Sanballat, Tobiah, Geshem the Arab, and the rest of our enemies heard that I had rebuilt the wall and not a gap was left—though to that time I had not yet installed the doors in the gates—Sanballat and Geshem sent me this message: 'Come, let us meet together in one of the villages on the plain of Ono.' But they were planning to harm me" (Nehemiah 6:1–2).

Tool #27. The Extension Cord of Grace: "My grace is sufficient for you, for my power is made perfect in weakness" (2 Corinthians 12:9).

Tool #28. The Goggles of Glory: "In the year that King Uzziah died, I had a vision of the LORD. He was on his throne high above, and his robe filled the temple" (Haggai 2:9 CEV).

Tool #29. The Jumper Cable of Divine Connection: "Who shall separate us from the love of God, shall tribulation, persecution, or famine, or peril or nakedness or sword?" (Romans 8:35).

Tool #30. The Knee Pads of Prayer and Fasting: "If my people, who are called by my name, will humble themselves and pray and seek my face and turn from their wicked ways, then I will hear from heaven, and I will forgive their sin and will heal their land" (2 Chronicles 7:14).

Tool #31. The Scaffolding of Healing: "Brothers and sisters, if someone is caught in a sin, you who live by the

Spirit should restore that person gently. But watch yourselves, or you also may tempted" (Galatians 6:1).

Tool #32. The Combination Square of Honesty: "Honest scales and balances belong to the LORD; all the weights in the bag are of his making" (Proverbs 16:11).

Tool #33. The Cable Ties of Marriage: "Therefore what God has joined together, let no one separate" (Mark 10:9).

Tool #34. The Adjustable Clamps of Relationships: "A friend loves at all times, and a brother is born for a time of adversity" (Proverbs 17:17).

Tool #35. The Anvil of God's Word: "But the word of the Lord endures forever." And this is the word that was preached to you" (1 Peter 1:27).

Tool #36. Sandpaper of Long Suffering: "I want to know Christ and experience the mighty power that raised him from the dead. I want to suffer with him, sharing in his death" (Philippians 2:10 NLT).

Tool #37. The Drill Bits of Perseverance: "Let perseverance finish its work so that you may be mature and complete, not lacking anything" (James 1:4).

Tool #38. The Soldering of the Holy Spirit: "And do not grieve the Holy Spirit of God, with whom you were sealed for the day of redemption" (Ephesians 4:30).

Tool #39. Electrical Tape of Trust: "Trust in the LORD with all your heart; do not depend on your own understanding" (Proverbs 3:5).

Tool #40. The Handsaw of Service: "To equip his people for works of service, so that the body of Christ may be built up" (Ephesians 4:12).

Tool #41. The Tool Belt of Truth: "Stand your ground, putting on the belt of truth and the body armor of God's righteousness" (Ephesians 6:14 NLT).

Tool #42. The Broom of New Beginnings: "See, I am doing a new thing! Now it springs up; do you not perceive it? I am making a way in the wilderness and streams in the wasteland" (Isaiah 43:19).

Tool #43. The Shovel of Success: "Study this Book of Instruction continually. Meditate on it day and night so you will be sure to obey everything written in it. Only then will you prosper and succeed in all you do" (Joshua 1:8 NLT).

Tool #44. The Scissors of Sanctification: "As far as the east is from the west, so far has He removed our transgressions from us" (Psalms 103:12 BSB).

Tool #45. The Wires of Worship: "Yet a time is coming and has now come when the true worshipers will worship the Father in the Spirit and in truth, for they are the kind of worshipers the Father seeks" (John 4:23).

Tool #46. The Shop Vac of Personal Cleansing: "Wash me thoroughly from my iniquity And cleanse me from my sin" (Psalms 51:2 NASB).

Tool #47. The Voltage Tester of Trials: "These trials will show that your faith is genuine. It is being tested as fire tests and purifies gold—though your faith is far more precious than mere gold. So when your faith remains strong through many trials, it will bring you much praise and glory and honor on the day when Jesus Christ is revealed to the whole world" (1 Peter 1:7 NLT).

Tool #48. The Water Hose of Hope: "Whoever believes in Me, as the Scripture has said: 'Streams of living water will flow from within him'" (John 7:38 BSB).

Tool #49. The Adjustable Wrench of Forgiveness: "For if we refuse to forgive others, our father will not forgive our sins" (Matthew 6:15 NLT).

Tool #50. The Helmet of Salvation: "Put on salvation as your helmet, and take the sword of the Spirit, which is the word of God" (Ephseians 6:17 NLT).

Tool #51. The WD–40 of Gladness: "To grant those who mourn in Zion, giving them a garland instead of ashes, the oil of gladness instead of mourning, the mantle of praise instead of a spirit of fainting. So, they will be called oaks of righteousness, the planting of the LORD, that He may be glorified" (Isaiah 61:3 NASB).

Tool #52. The Gorilla Glue of the Family: "As for me and my house, we will serve the Lord" (Joshua 24:15).

REFERENCES

Notes

1. Ranier, Thom S. "Six Stages of a Dying Church." *ThomRanier.com.* June 12, 2017. https://web.archive.org/web/20181129231551/https://thomrainer.com/2017/06/six-stages-dying-church.

2. McGillicuddy, Cassidy. "Wait, HOW Many Churches Close Per Year?" *Patheos.com.* November 29, 2018. https://www.patheos.com/blogs/rolltodisbelieve/2018/11/29/how-many-churches-close-per-year.

3. Easlum, Bill. "Too Many Pastors Are Wasting Their Lives." *The Effective Church Group.* February 19, 2016. http://effectivechurch.com/too-many-pastors-are-wasting-their-lives.

4. "Nine Important Church Statistics for 2017." *ReachRight.* https://reachrightstudios.com/9-important-church-statistics-2017.

5. "Niles Is Named One of Best Places to Raise a Family." *Chicago Parent.* December 16, 2010.

https://www.chicagoparent.com/archives/niles-named-one-best-places-raise-family.

6. "The Cost of US Wars Then and Now." *War History Online.* October 5, 2016. https://www.warhistory online.com/history/cost-u-s-wars-now.html.

7. Wilson, R. Dick. "Nehemiah." *International Standard Bible Encyclopedia Online.* Edited by James Orr. William B. Eerdmans Publishing Co., 1939. https://www.internationalstandardbible.com/N/nehe miah.html.

8. Kidner, Derek. "Ezra and Nehemiah." *Tyndale Old Testament Commentaries.* Intervarsity Press, 1979.

9. Williamson, H.G.M. "Ezra, Nehemiah." *Word Bible Commentary.* Word, 1985, p. 172.

10. Williamson, "Ezra, Nehemiah."

11. Fensham, Charles F. *The Books of Ezra and Nehemiah.* William B. Eerdmans Publishing Co., 1982, p. 134.

12. Picchi, Aimee. "Facebook: Your Personal Info for Sale." *CBS News.* April 8, 2018. https://www.cbsnews.com/news/facebook-your-personal-info-for-sale.

13. Gaebelein, Frank E. and Geoffrey W. Grogan. *The Expositor's Bible Commentary.* Zondervan, 1988, p. 690.

14. Willmington, Harald L. *The Outline Bible.* Tyndale House Publishers, 1999.

15. Gaebelein, Frank E. and Geoffrey W. Grogan. *The Expositor's Bible Commentary*. Zondervan, 1988, p. 722–723.

16. Plueddmann, James E. *Leading Across Cultures*. *InterVarsity Press*, 2009.

17. Barach, John. *Twelve Sermons on Nehemiah*. Athanasius Press, 2011, p. 33–35.

18. Florida Department of Health. *FL Health Charts*. http://www.flhealthcharts.com/charts/default.aspx.

19. Barach, *Twelve Sermons on Nehemiah*.

20. Barach, *Twelve Sermons on Nehemiah*, p. 634.

About the Author

Christopher A. Lewis is married to Annette, and together they have two children, Christiana and Alexander. Christopher is the lead Pastor of Christian Community Church of God in Lauderhill, Florida.

Bishop C. A. Lewis received a bachelor's in ministry with an emphasis on cross-cultural evangelism from the National Bible College, a master's in theological studies with an emphasis in urban ministry from Trinity International University and is currently pursuing his Doctor of Ministry at South Florida Bible College and Seminary.

At the age of 17, Christopher surrendered his life to Jesus Christ. He started his ministry traveling throughout Guyana ministering as a musician, worship leader, and revival speaker. His ministry expanded to include weekly healing and miracles services, revivals, and evangelistic crusades throughout the Caribbean, United States, United Kingdom, Canada, and Africa, and he has also appeared as a featured guest on several international radio and television programs, including TBN.

Bishop Lewis can be contacted through email: c.lewis6@comcast.net.

62732505R00076

Made in the USA
Columbia, SC
05 July 2019